THE PHILLIP KEVEREN SERIES EASY PIANO

RAGTIME CLASSICS

— PIANO LEVEL —
EARLY INTERMEDIATE/INTERMEDIATE
(HLSPL LEVEL 4-5)

ISBN 978-1-4234-0784-3

HAL•LEONARD®
CORPORATION
7777 W. BLUEMOUND RD. P.O. BOX 13819 MILWAUKEE, WI 53213

In Australia Contact:
Hal Leonard Australia Pty. Ltd.
4 Lentara Court
Cheltenham, Victoria, 3192 Australia
Email: ausadmin@halleonard.com

For all works contained herein:
Unauthorized copying, arranging, adapting, recording or public performance is an infringement of copyright.
Infringers are liable under the law.

Visit Hal Leonard Online at
www.halleonard.com

PREFACE

The playful sounds of ragtime music are loved by people of all ages. However, playing the original scores at the piano can be a challenge for the developing pianist, and that is where this collection of arrangements comes in. My goal was to create settings that accurately capture the spirit of these compositions, yet simplify the technical demands to allow pianists to play them earlier in their learning experience.

My only advice regarding the performance of these pieces would be the same instruction Scott Joplin gave us for "The Entertainer": NOT FAST. The syncopated charm that distinguishes ragtime comes through best at a moderate march tempo.

Sincerely,
Phillip Keveren

BIOGRAPHY

Phillip Keveren, a multi-talented keyboard artist and composer, has composed original works in a variety of genres from piano solo to symphonic orchestra. Mr. Keveren gives frequent concerts and workshops for teachers and their students in the United States, Canada, Europe, and Asia. Mr. Keveren holds a B.M. in composition from California State University Northridge and a M.M. in composition from the University of Southern California.

CONTENTS

ANTOINETTE

By SCOTT JOPLIN
Arranged by Phillip Keveren

March tempo

Copyright © 2006 by HAL LEONARD CORPORATION
International Copyright Secured   All Rights Reserved

BOHEMIA

By JOSEPH F. LAMB
Arranged by Phillip Keveren

March tempo

Copyright © 2006 by HAL LEONARD CORPORATION
International Copyright Secured   All Rights Reserved

TRIO

THE CASCADES

By SCOTT JOPLIN
Arranged by Phillip Keveren

March tempo

Copyright © 2006 by HAL LEONARD CORPORATION
International Copyright Secured   All Rights Reserved

CHAMPAGNE RAG

By JOSEPH F. LAMB
Arranged by Phillip Keveren

Copyright © 2006 by HAL LEONARD CORPORATION
International Copyright Secured All Rights Reserved

CHROMATIC RAG

By WILL HELD
Arranged by Phillip Keveren

Playfully

Copyright © 2006 by HAL LEONARD CORPORATION
International Copyright Secured   All Rights Reserved

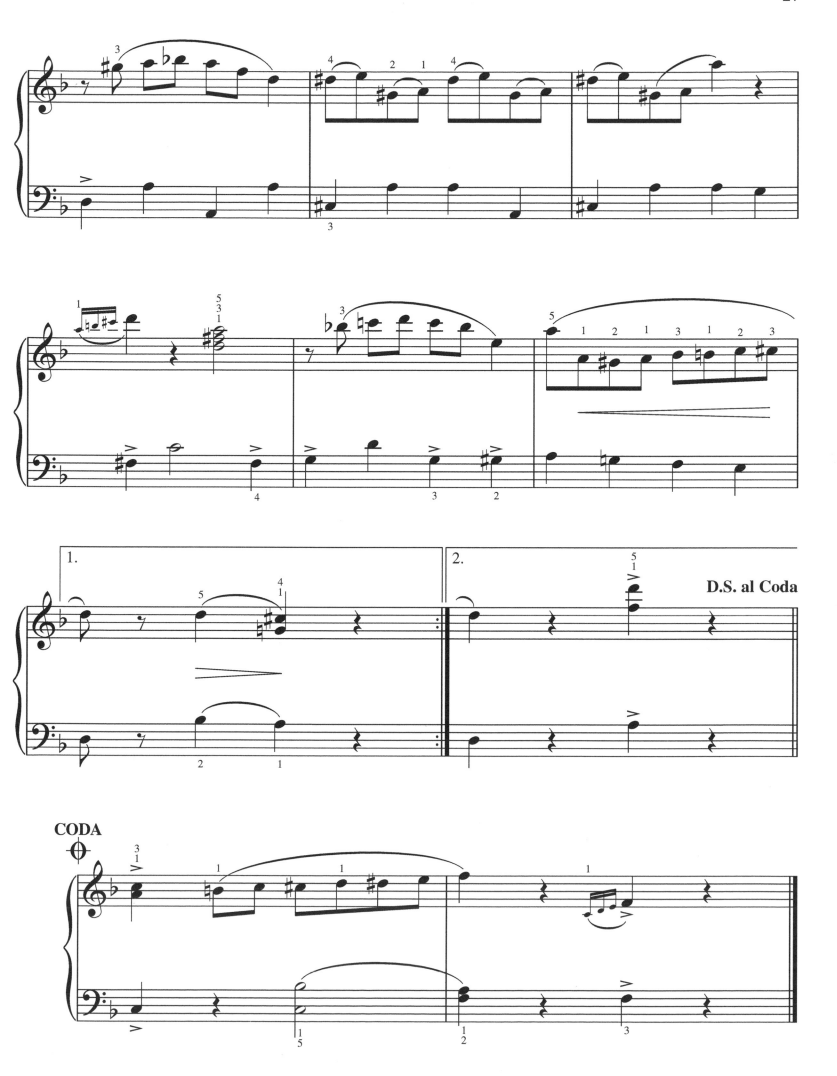

DIMPLES

By L.E. COLBURN
Arranged by Phillip Keveren

March tempo

Copyright © 2006 by HAL LEONARD CORPORATION
International Copyright Secured   All Rights Reserved

THE EASY WINNERS

By SCOTT JOPLIN
Arranged by Phillip Keveren

Copyright © 2006 by HAL LEONARD CORPORATION
International Copyright Secured   All Rights Reserved

THE ENTERTAINER

By SCOTT JOPLIN
Arranged by Phillip Keveren

Copyright © 2006 by HAL LEONARD CORPORATION
International Copyright Secured   All Rights Reserved

THE FASCINATOR

By JAMES SCOTT
Arranged by Phillip Keveren

Copyright © 2006 by HAL LEONARD CORPORATION
International Copyright Secured   All Rights Reserved

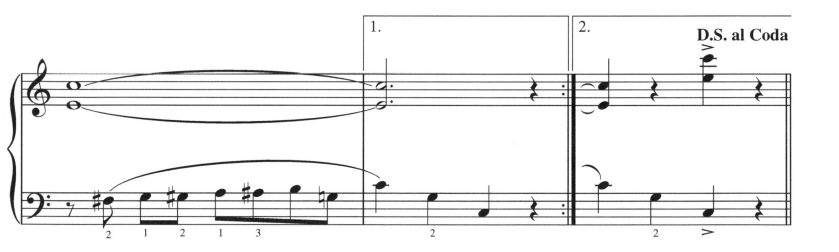

D.S. al Coda

1.

2.

CODA

HARLEM RAG

By TOM TURPIN
Arranged by Phillip Keveren

March tempo

Copyright © 2006 by HAL LEONARD CORPORATION
International Copyright Secured   All Rights Reserved

MAPLE LEAF RAG

By SCOTT JOPLIN
Arranged by Phillip Keveren

Copyright © 2006 by HAL LEONARD CORPORATION
International Copyright Secured   All Rights Reserved

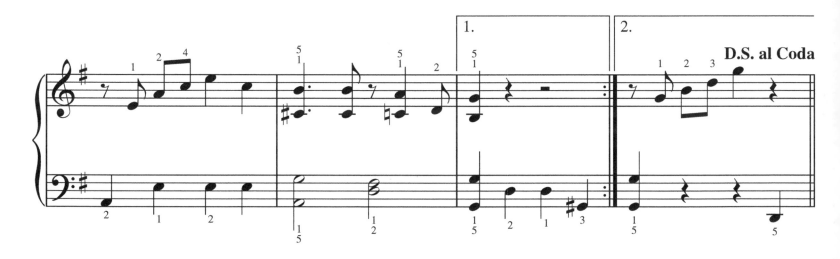

D.S. al Coda

CODA

RAG TIME CHIMES

By PERCY WENRICH
Arranged by Phillip Keveren

Copyright © 2006 by HAL LEONARD CORPORATION
International Copyright Secured   All Rights Reserved

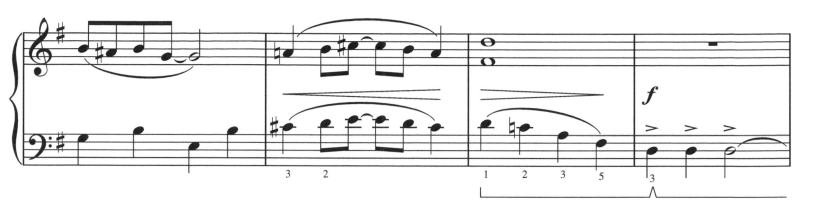

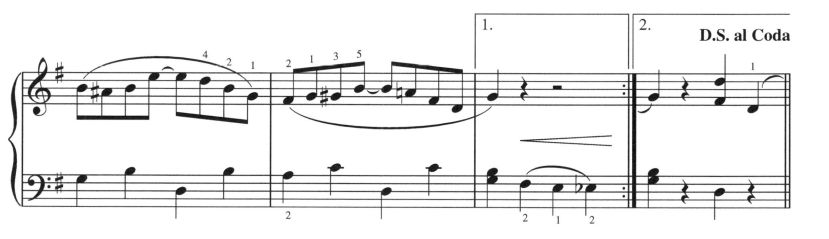

D.S. al Coda

CODA

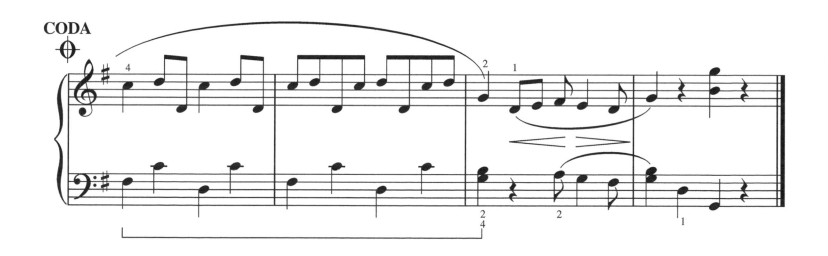

REINDEER RAG

By JOSEPH F. LAMB
Arranged by Phillip Keveren

Moderate prance

Copyright © 2006 by HAL LEONARD CORPORATION
International Copyright Secured   All Rights Reserved

To Coda ⊕

A TENNESSEE TANTALIZER

By CHARLES HUNTER
Arranged by Phillip Keveren

Steady as she goes

Copyright © 2006 by HAL LEONARD CORPORATION
International Copyright Secured   All Rights Reserved

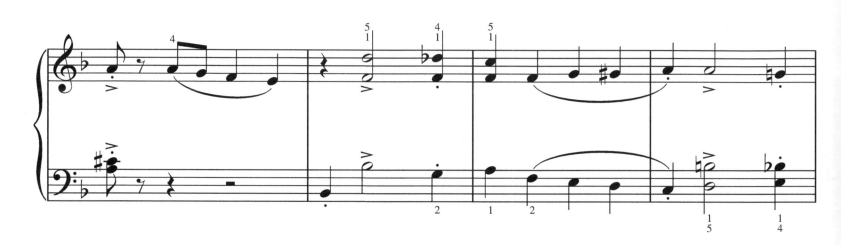

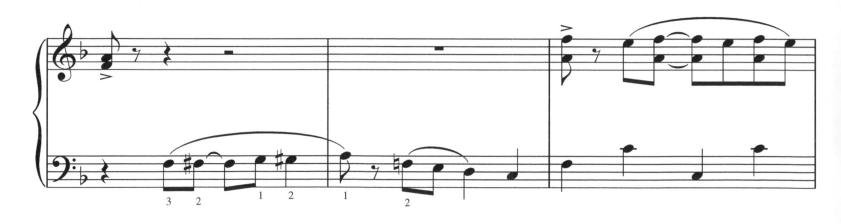

SENSATION

By JOSEPH F. LAMB
Arranged by Phillip Keveren

March tempo

Copyright © 2006 by HAL LEONARD CORPORATION
International Copyright Secured   All Rights Reserved

D.C. al Fine
(without repeat)

TWELFTH STREET RAG

By EUDAY L. BOWMAN
Arranged by Phillip Keveren

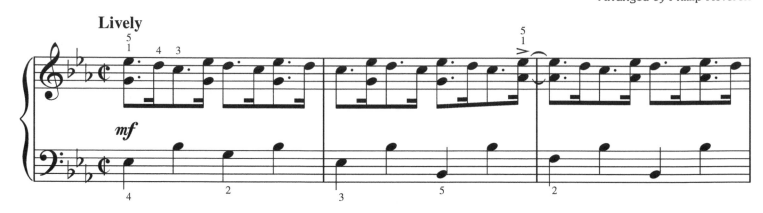

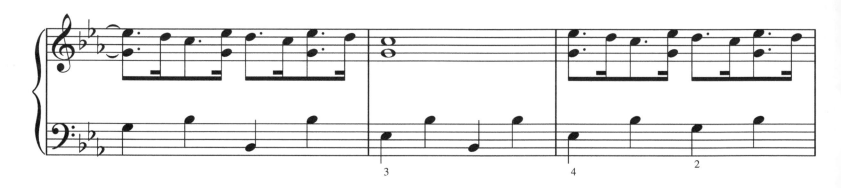

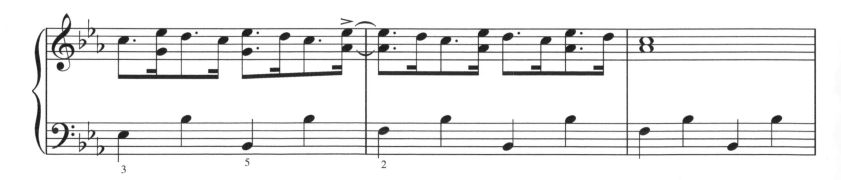

Copyright © 2006 by HAL LEONARD CORPORATION
International Copyright Secured   All Rights Reserved

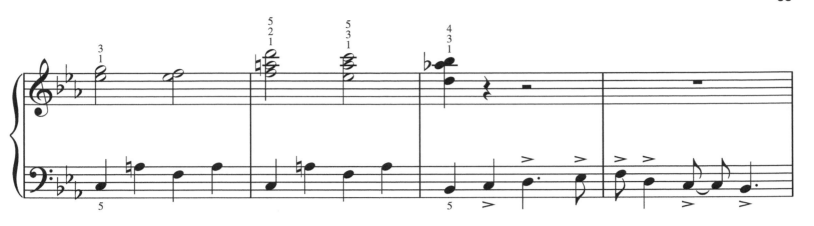

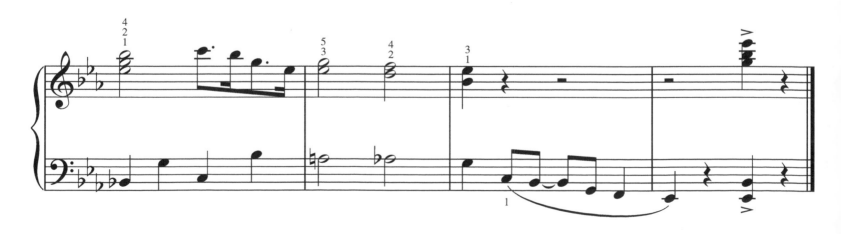

WILD CHERRIES RAG

By TED SNYDER
Arranged by Phillip Keveren

March tempo

Copyright © 2006 by HAL LEONARD CORPORATION
International Copyright Secured   All Rights Reserved

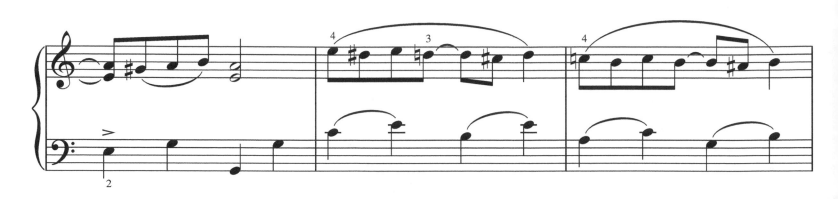

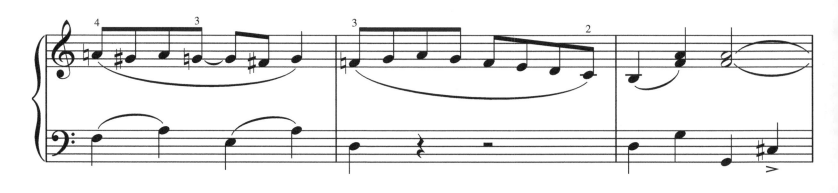

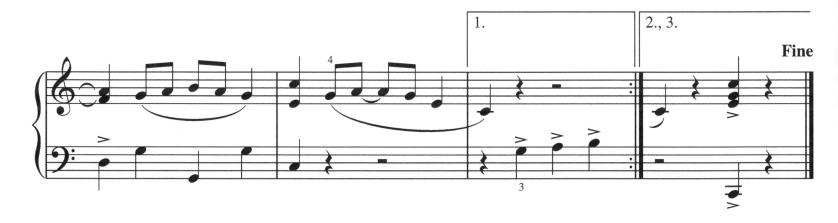

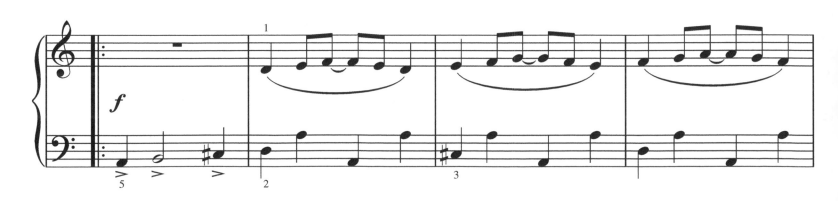

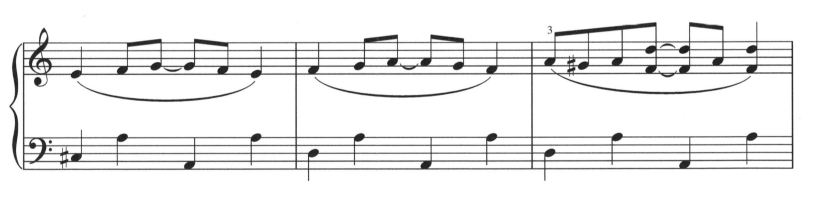

1.

2. **D.S. al Fine**
(take 2nd ending)

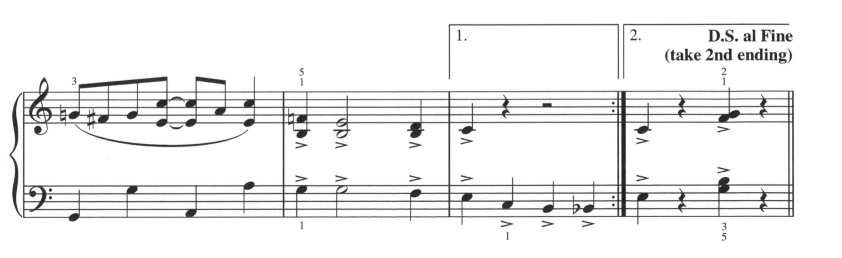

THE PHILLIP KEVEREN SERIES

HAL•LEONARD®

Search songlists, more products and place your order from your favorite music retailer at **halleonard.com**

Disney characters and artwork
TM & © 2021 Disney LLC

PIANO SOLO

00156644	**ABBA for Classical Piano**	$15.99
00311024	**Above All**	$12.99
00311348	**Americana**	$12.99
00198473	**Bach Meets Jazz**	$14.99
00313594	**Bacharach and David**	$15.99
00306412	**The Beatles**	$19.99
00312189	**The Beatles for Classical Piano**	$17.99
00275876	**The Beatles – Recital Suites**	$19.99
00312546	**Best Piano Solos**	$15.99
00156601	**Blessings**	$14.99
00198656	**Blues Classics**	$14.99
00284359	**Broadway Songs with a Classical Flair**	$14.99
00310669	**Broadway's Best**	$16.99
00312106	**Canzone Italiana**	$12.99
00280848	**Carpenters**	$17.99
00310629	**A Celtic Christmas**	$14.99
00310549	**The Celtic Collection**	$14.99
00280571	**Celtic Songs with a Classical Flair**	$12.99
00263362	**Charlie Brown Favorites**	$14.99
00312190	**Christmas at the Movies**	$15.99
00294754	**Christmas Carols with a Classical Flair**	$12.99
00311414	**Christmas Medleys**	$14.99
00236669	**Christmas Praise Hymns**	$12.99
00233788	**Christmas Songs for Classical Piano**	$14.99
00311769	**Christmas Worship Medleys**	$14.99
00310607	**Cinema Classics**	$15.99
00301857	**Circles**	$10.99
00311101	**Classic Wedding Songs**	$12.99
00311292	**Classical Folk**	$10.95
00311083	**Classical Jazz**	$14.99
00137779	**Coldplay for Classical Piano**	$16.99
00311103	**Contemporary Wedding Songs**	$12.99
00348788	**Country Songs with a Classical Flair**	$14.99
00249097	**Disney Recital Suites**	$17.99
00311754	**Disney Songs for Classical Piano**	$17.99
00241379	**Disney Songs for Ragtime Piano**	$17.99
00364812	**The Essential Hymn Anthology**	$34.99
00311881	**Favorite Wedding Songs**	$14.99
00315974	**Fiddlin' at the Piano**	$12.99
00311811	**The Film Score Collection**	$15.99
00269408	**Folksongs with a Classical Flair**	$12.99
00144353	**The Gershwin Collection**	$14.99
00233789	**Golden Scores**	$14.99
00144351	**Gospel Greats**	$14.99
00183566	**The Great American Songbook**	$14.99
00312084	**The Great Melodies**	$14.99
00311157	**Great Standards**	$14.99
00171621	**A Grown-Up Christmas List**	$14.99
00311071	**The Hymn Collection**	$14.99
00311349	**Hymn Medleys**	$14.99
00280705	**Hymns in a Celtic Style**	$14.99
00269407	**Hymns with a Classical Flair**	$14.99
00311249	**Hymns with a Touch of Jazz**	$14.99
00310905	**I Could Sing of Your Love Forever**	$16.99
00310762	**Jingle Jazz**	$15.99
00175310	**Billy Joel for Classical Piano**	$16.99
00126449	**Elton John for Classical Piano**	$19.99
00310839	**Let Freedom Ring!**	$12.99
00238988	**Andrew Lloyd Webber Piano Songbook**	$14.99
00313227	**Andrew Lloyd Webber Solos**	$17.99
00313523	**Mancini Magic**	$16.99
00312113	**More Disney Songs for Classical Piano**	$16.99
00311295	**Motown Hits**	$14.99
00300640	**Piano Calm**	$12.99
00339131	**Piano Calm: Christmas**	$14.99
00346009	**Piano Calm: Prayer**	$14.99
00306870	**Piazzolla Tangos**	$17.99
00386709	**Praise and Worship for Classical Piano**	$14.99
00156645	**Queen for Classical Piano**	$17.99
00310755	**Richard Rodgers Classics**	$17.99
00289545	**Scottish Songs**	$12.99
00119403	**The Sound of Music**	$16.99
00311978	**The Spirituals Collection**	$12.99
00366023	**So Far...**	$14.99
00210445	**Star Wars**	$16.99
00224738	**Symphonic Hymns for Piano**	$14.99
00366022	**Three-Minute Encores**	$16.99
00279673	**Tin Pan Alley**	$12.99
00312112	**Treasured Hymns for Classical Piano**	$15.99
00144926	**The Twelve Keys of Christmas**	$14.99
00278486	**The Who for Classical Piano**	$16.99
00294036	**Worship with a Touch of Jazz**	$14.99
00311911	**Yuletide Jazz**	$19.99

EASY PIANO

00210401	**Adele for Easy Classical Piano**	$17.99
00310610	**African-American Spirituals**	$12.99
00218244	**The Beatles for Easy Classical Piano**	$14.99
00218387	**Catchy Songs for Piano**	$12.99
00310973	**Celtic Dreams**	$12.99
00233686	**Christmas Carols for Easy Classical Piano**	$14.99
00311126	**Christmas Pops**	$16.99
00368199	**Christmas Reflections**	$14.99
00311548	**Classic Pop/Rock Hits**	$14.99
00310769	**A Classical Christmas**	$14.99
00310975	**Classical Movie Themes**	$12.99
00144352	**Disney Songs for Easy Classical Piano**	$14.99
00311093	**Early Rock 'n' Roll**	$14.99
00311997	**Easy Worship Medleys**	$14.99
00289547	**Duke Ellington**	$14.99
00160297	**Folksongs for Easy Classical Piano**	$12.99

00110374	**George Gershwin Classics**	$14.99
00310805	**Gospel Treasures**	$14.99
00306821	**Vince Guaraldi Collection**	$19.99
00160294	**Hymns for Easy Classical Piano**	$14.99
00310798	**Immortal Hymns**	$12.99
00311294	**Jazz Standards**	$12.99
00355474	**Living Hope**	$14.99
00310744	**Love Songs**	$14.99
00233740	**The Most Beautiful Songs for Easy Classical Piano**	$12.99
00220036	**Pop Ballads**	$14.99
00311406	**Pop Gems of the 1950s**	$12.95
00233739	**Pop Standards for Easy Classical Piano**	$12.99
00102887	**A Ragtime Christmas**	$12.99
00311293	**Ragtime Classics**	$14.99
00312028	**Santa Swings**	$14.99
00233688	**Songs from Childhood for Easy Classical Piano**	$12.99
00103258	**Songs of Inspiration**	$14.99
00310840	**Sweet Land of Liberty**	$12.99
00126450	**10,000 Reasons**	$16.99
00310712	**Timeless Praise**	$14.99
00311086	**TV Themes**	$14.99
00310717	**21 Great Classics**	$14.99
00160076	**Waltzes & Polkas for Easy Classical Piano**	$12.99
00145342	**Weekly Worship**	$17.99

BIG-NOTE PIANO

00310838	**Children's Favorite Movie Songs**	$14.99
00346000	**Christmas Movie Magic**	$12.99
00277368	**Classical Favorites**	$12.99
00277370	**Disney Favorites**	$14.99
00310888	**Joy to the World**	$12.99
00310908	**The Nutcracker**	$12.99
00277371	**Star Wars**	$16.99

BEGINNING PIANO SOLOS

00311202	**Awesome God**	$14.99
00310837	**Christian Children's Favorites**	$14.99
00311117	**Christmas Traditions**	$10.99
00311250	**Easy Hymns**	$12.99
00102710	**Everlasting God**	$10.99
00311403	**Jazzy Tunes**	$10.95
00310822	**Kids' Favorites**	$12.99
00367778	**A Magical Christmas**	$14.99
00338175	**Silly Songs for Kids**	$9.99

PIANO DUET

00126452	**The Christmas Variations**	$14.99
00362562	**Classic Piano Duets**	$14.99
00311350	**Classical Theme Duets**	$12.99
00295099	**Gospel Duets**	$12.99
00311544	**Hymn Duets**	$14.99
00311203	**Praise & Worship Duets**	$14.99
00294755	**Sacred Christmas Duets**	$14.99
00119405	**Star Wars**	$16.99
00253545	**Worship Songs for Two**	$12.99

Prices, contents, and availability subject to change without notice.

0422

158

It's Easy to Play Your Favorite Songs with Hal Leonard Easy Piano Books

The Best Praise & Worship Songs Ever

The name says it all: over 70 of the best P&W songs today. Titles include: Awesome God • Blessed Be Your Name • Come, Now Is the Time to Worship • Days of Elijah • Here I Am to Worship • Open the Eyes of My Heart • Shout to the Lord • We Fall Down • and more.
00311312 .... $19.99

First 50 Popular Songs You Should Play on the Piano

50 great pop classics for beginning pianists to learn, including: Candle in the Wind • Chopsticks • Don't Know Why • Hallelujah • Happy Birthday to You • Heart and Soul • I Walk the Line • Just the Way You Are • Let It Be • Let It Go • Over the Rainbow • Piano Man • and many more.
00131140 .... $16.99

The Greatest Video Game Music

28 easy piano selections for the music that envelops you as you lose yourself in the world of video games, including: Angry Birds Theme • Assassin's Creed Revelations • Dragonborn (Skyrim Theme) • Elder Scrolls: Oblivion • Minecraft: Sweden • Rage of Sparta from God of War III • and more.
00202545 .... $17.99

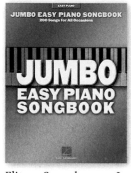

Jumbo Easy Piano Songbook

200 classical favorites, folk songs and jazz standards. Includes: Amazing Grace • Beale Street Blues • Bridal Chorus • Buffalo Gals • Canon in D • Cielito Lindo • Danny Boy • The Entertainer • Für Elise • Greensleeves • Jamaica Farewell • Marianne • Molly Malone • Ode to Joy • Peg O' My Heart • Rockin' Robin • Yankee Doodle • dozens more!
00311014 .... $19.99

Songs from A Star Is Born, The Greatest Showman, La La Land, and More Movie Musicals

Movie musical lovers will delight in this songbook chock full of top-notch songs arranged for easy piano with lyrics from blockbuster movies. Includes: City of Stars from *La La Land* • Suddenly from *Les Misérables* • This Is Me from *The Greatest Showman* • Shallow from *A Star Is Born* • and more.
00287577 .... $17.99

50 Easy Classical Themes

Easy arrangements of 50 classical tunes representing more than 30 composers, including: Bach, Beethoven, Chopin, Debussy, Dvorak, Handel, Haydn, Liszt, Mozart, Mussorgsky, Puccini, Rossini, Schubert, Strauss, Tchaikovsky, Vivaldi, and more.
00311215 .... $14.99

Pop Songs for Kids

Kids from all corners of the world love and sing along to the songs of Taylor Swift, One Direction, Katy Perry, and other pop stars. This collection features 25 songs from these and many more artists in easy piano format. Includes: Brave • Can't Stop the Feeling • Firework • Home • Let It Go • Shake It Off • What Makes You Beautiful • and more.
00221920 .... $14.99

Simple Songs – The Easiest Easy Piano Songs

Play 50 of your favorite songs in the easiest of arrangements! Songs include: Castle on a Cloud • Do-Re-Mi • Happy Birthday to You • Hey Jude • Let It Go • Linus and Lucy • Over the Rainbow • Smile • Star Wars (Main Theme) • Tomorrow • and more.
00142041 .... $14.99

VH1's 100 Greatest Songs of Rock and Roll

The results from the VH1 show that featured the 100 greatest rock and roll songs of all time are here in this awesome collection! Songs include: Born to Run • Good Vibrations • Hey Jude • Hotel California • Imagine • Light My Fire • Like a Rolling Stone • Respect • and more.
00311110 .... $29.99

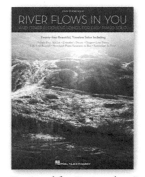

River Flows in You and Other Eloquent Songs for Easy Piano Solo

24 piano favorites arranged so that even beginning players can sound great. Includes: All of Me • Bella's Lullaby • Cristofori's Dream • Il Postino (The Postman) • Jessica's Theme (Breaking in the Colt) • The John Dunbar Theme • and more.
00137581 .... $14.99

Disney's My First Song Book

16 favorite songs to sing and play. Every page is beautifully illustrated with full-color art from Disney features. Songs include: Beauty and the Beast • Bibbidi-Bobbidi-Boo • Circle of Life • Cruella De Vil • A Dream Is a Wish Your Heart Makes • Hakuna Matata • Under the Sea • Winnie the Pooh • You've Got a Friend in Me • and more.
00310322 .... $17.99

Top Hits of 2019

20 of the year's best are included in this collection arranged for easy piano with lyrics. Includes: Bad Guy (Billie Eilish) • I Don't Care (Ed Sheeran & Justin Bieber) • ME! (Taylor Swift feat. Brendon Urie) • Old Town Road (Remix) (Lil Nas X feat. Billy Ray Cyrus) • Senorita (Shawn Mendes & Camila Cabello) • Someone You Loved (Lewis Capaldi) • and more.
00302273 .... $16.99

Get complete song lists and more at
www.halleonard.com

Prices, contents, and availability subject to change without notice
Disney characters and artwork © Disney Enterprises, Inc.

HAL•LEONARD

0320
239